THE WAY
GOD FIGHTS

PEACE·AND·JUSTICE·SERIES 1

THE WAY GOD FIGHTS

War and Peace in the Old Testament

LOIS BARRETT

HERALD PRESS
Scottdale, Pennsylvania
Kitchener, Ontario
1987

Library of Congress Cataloging-in-Publication Data

Barrett, Lois.
    The way God fights.

    (The Peace and justice series ; 1)
    Bibliography: p.
    1. War—Biblical teaching.   2. Peace—Biblical
teaching.   3. Bible.   O.T.—Criticism, interpretation,
etc.   I. Title.   II. Series.
BS1199.W2B37   1987   261.8'73   87-11936
ISBN 0-8361-3447-8 (pbk.)

The cover illustration is from *Jericho*, an etching by Julius Schnorr von
Carolsfeld, c. 1850.

Scripture references are from the *Good News Bible*.
Old Testament: Copyright © American Bible Society 1976;
New Testament: Copyright © American Bible Society 1966, 1971, 1976.

THE WAY GOD FIGHTS

Copyright © 1987 by Herald Press, Scottdale, Pa. 15683
        Published simultaneously in Canada by Herald Press,
        Kitchener, Ont. N2G 4M5. All rights reserved.
Library of Congress Catalog Card Number: 87-11936
International Standard Book Number: 0-8361-3447-8
Printed in the United States of America
Design by Gwen M. Stamm

87 88 89 90 91 92 93 94 95 96 10 9 8 7 6 5 4 3 2 1

To Millard Lind,
who helped me love
the Old Testament

Contents

Foreword

War and peace touch our lives in one way or another. Our governments may tax us to help pay for military training, guns, tanks, fighter planes, or missiles. We may be asked to serve in the armed forces of our country, whose leaders teach people how to kill others.

Is there not a better way to resolve conflict? How can we end anger, hatred, and injustice; work for justice and righteousness, and security for all nations; thereby establishing peace? The author shows first how God worked in Old Testament times. She explains the concept of holy war as God's way of helping the people of faith. The key to victory was faith in God, not military might. God did the fighting. Faith and obedience were required so God could bring about the victory.

But God as warrior is only one of the images the Bible uses to describe God. Others include wind, fire, light, shepherd, potter, mother eagle, and hostess. "The Old Testament tells us that we do not need to try to have a strong army," the author states. "We can trust in the power of God, not in human violence" to overcome conflict.

The writer challenges the notion that the Old Testament supports warfare. She shows how God called the people of Israel away from the futility of human violence, to trust in the power of God to overcome evil. She also shows how the New Testament builds on this principle of trusting God to overcome our enemies.

The Way God Fights is volume one in the Peace and Justice Series listed inside the back cover. It was commissioned by Mennonite Board of Missions, Mennonite Publishing House, and the peace sections of the Board of Congregational Ministries and Mennonite Central Committee—all Mennonite agencies. The goal is to bridge the gap between scholarly Mennonite writings and the narrowly focused evangelical literature that talks peace while supporting warfare. Persons wanting to pursue the theme further may check the references listed "For More Serious Study" near the end of the book.

—J. Allen Brubaker, Editor
Peace and Justice Series

PART ONE

War and Peace
in the Old Testament

CHAPTER 1

Holy War as God's War

As we read the Bible, we find both war and peace. We see Jesus, who said, "Love your enemies" (Matthew 5:44). We see Jesus letting himself be killed; not letting his disciples fight back with swords when he was arrested (John 18:10-11, 36).

We read in the book of Isaiah of a new king who would rule his people with justice. There would be such peace that even wolves and sheep would live together in peace (Isaiah 11:1-9). Isaiah asked the people of Judah not to depend on help from the Egyptian armies to defend their country, but to depend on God. "Come back and quietly trust in me. Then you will be strong and secure," God told the people (Isaiah 30:15).

Yet we also read in the Old Testament of God as a warrior (Exodus 15:3). We read of God commanding Israel to go to war against the Canaanite cities and to kill all the people who lived there. (See Joshua 8.) How could the God who loved peace also command war? We know that Jesus was peaceful and wanted to save all people. How can he be the Son of a God who seemed to want to kill the enemy?

Christians through the ages have offered many answers to these questions. Some have said, "We believe in Jesus as a person of love and peace. God's mind must have changed. God told the nation of Israel to do one thing. Now, through Jesus, God is telling us something different."

Others have said, "There is no way to put together the God of love in the New Testament and the God of war in the Old Testament. So we will not pay any attention to the Old Testament. We will just read the New Testament."

Still others have said, "Both the New Testament and the Old Testament tell us the right things to do. Jesus teaches people to act in peace with each other one to one, but Jesus does not say anything about how nations and rulers should act. We will follow Jesus and live in peace with the people we know. But we will let the nation go to war, because God let the nation of Israel do that."

Or others have said, "The Bible tells how people of faith saw themselves and God relating to each other. In early Israel, the people did not understand God as well as the prophets or Jesus or Paul. Human beings have understood God better and better as time goes on. Now we understand that God wants peace, even though the people of early Israel thought God wanted war."

None of these ideas really answers the question for us. It would be easier to find an answer if we could say that the Old Testament is full of war and the New Testament is full of peace. But it does not work out quite so neatly. Even in the New Testament, we find ideas about war. In the book of Revelation, we find the war of the Lamb, who wins out over the forces of evil. Jesus himself used the battle cry of the Old Testament: "Do not be afraid. I am with you." His mother Mary's song of praise (Luke 1:46-55) expected that

Jesus would bring down mighty kings from their thrones and lift up the lowly.

In the Old Testament, the prophets saw peace in the future. God helped Gideon's army defeat the Midianites by using trumpets and jars, not spears and other weapons! And in the Old Testament, God is called Lord of Hosts (that is, Lord of Armies) more times in the books of the prophets than in the books about earlier times. How do we put together the different ideas about war and peace that we find in the Bible, but especially in the Old Testament? How can we worship God the Warrior and the Prince of Peace?

We cannot just throw out the Old Testament. Without the Old Testament, we cannot understand the New Testament. Without the history of the Jewish people, we cannot understand Jesus, a Jew. Jesus, himself, said, "Do not think that I have come to do away with the Law of Moses and the teachings of the prophets. I have not come to do away with them, but to make their teachings come true" (Matthew 5:17).

Also, when we study the Old Testament with care, we find that it does not say war is always good. The Old Testament does not always lift up the soldier or the king. In fact, we find that God wanted only a certain kind of war. That kind of war is sometimes called "holy war." It is "holy" because it is God's war, not people's war.

CHAPTER 2

The Exodus as God's War

The most important "holy war" in the Old Testament is the Exodus (the going out) of the Hebrew people from Egypt. Every part of the Old Testament—the Law, the Prophets, the Writings—speaks about the Exodus. The people of Israel saw the Exodus as the most important happening in their life as a nation. They celebrated the Exodus during the Passover season every year. They saw the Exodus as the best example of how God had acted to save them.

Psalm 105:43-45 remembered:

> So [God] led his chosen people out, and they sang and shouted for joy. He gave them the lands of other peoples and let them take over their fields, so that his people would obey his laws and keep all his commands. Praise the LORD!

In the Exodus, the Hebrew slaves in Egypt escaped— not by their own actions, but by God's actions. God sent the locusts, flies, and other disasters to Egypt. These things convinced Pharaoh, the king of Egypt, to let the Hebrew slaves go. Then Pharaoh changed his mind and pursued the Hebrews with his armies in their fast chariots. But God sent a wind to roll back the waters of the Red Sea so the Hebrew people could cross over and get away from the army of Egypt. But the soldiers and their horses drowned when they tried to follow.

The Song of Moses in Exodus 15 celebrated the actions of God, not human heroes:

> I will sing to the LORD because he has won a glorious victory; he has thrown the horses and their riders into the sea. The LORD is my strong defender; he is the one who has saved me. He is my God and I will praise him, my fathers' God, and I will sing about his greatness. The LORD is a warrior; the LORD [Yahweh] is his name.

> (The *Good News Bible* uses LORD for the Hebrew name of God, Yahweh.)

The people of Israel became a nation because God fought for them, not because they fought for themselves. In fact, they had been a people without a country, a people without an army or weapons. Weapons had not been necessary. The people needed only to trust that God would win for them. In Exodus 14:13-14, Moses told the people,

> Don't be afraid! Stand your ground, and you will see what the LORD will do to save you today; you will never see these Egyptians again. The LORD will fight for you, and all you have to do is keep still.

The Song of Moses (Exodus 15) is one of the oldest parts of the Old Testament. Its style and language show us that it was written about the twelfth century B.C. That was about the same time as the Exodus took place. The idea of God being the only one who should fight for Israel is a very old idea. It is not something that was written into the Scriptures later, after the people of God had learned it was wrong for them to kill. It does not begin with the prophets. It was there from the beginning of Israel.

The attitude that we do not need to fight, but can trust God to save us, appears in the stories about the ancestors of Israel. Abraham believed that God would give him the land, and he did not need to fight for it. Because he trusted in the promise of God, Abraham was ready to let his nephew Lot take the best land rather than fight with him (Genesis 13:14ff.). Isaac freely gave water rights to Abimelech, the king of Gerar, without fighting (Genesis 26:1-33). Jacob was willing to offer himself and his people as servants to his brother Esau, rather than fight (Genesis 32—33).

Then, in the Exodus from Egypt, the people of Israel saw that when they trusted in God, God would save them. The miracles of God showed everyone that God was a Ruler who was greater than even the king of Egypt. The God of Israel, Yahweh, was a Warrior who could save his people from their enemies now, within history. Yahweh had the power to save them, even if the people of Israel themselves did no fighting at all.

The event of the Exodus became the best example of holy war in the Old Testament. The people of Israel used the language of war (the salvation language that they knew) to describe what God had done for them. God had done miracles ("signs and wonders") before Pharaoh to free the people of Israel from slavery. God had caused the enemy to "tremble," "be dismayed," "melt away," and be filled with "terror and dread." These words were all part of war language in the ancient Near East.

Moses had led them into battle with the words, "Do not be afraid." This was the cry that began a battle. The language of war took on new meaning. This language did not describe fighting by Israel, but the action of God to win victory for Israel. This was war language, but it was used in a new way.

CHAPTER 3

The Conquest as God's War

When the people of Israel ended their journey from Egypt through the desert, they entered the land of Canaan. The stories of the first years that Israel lived in Canaan are told in the books of Joshua and Judges. These books are full of stories about war.

These stories show the tribes of Israel fighting the cities and tribes that already lived in Canaan. Many stories show these battles as bloody. Sometimes the armies of Israel killed all the people who lived in an enemy city.

Often this killing was seen as something which God had commanded them to do. Joshua told his army before they took the city of Jericho, "The LORD has given you the city! The city and everything in it must be totally destroyed as an offering to the LORD" (Joshua 6:16). Joshua 10:40, 42 says,

> Joshua conquered the whole land. He defeated the kings of the hill country, the eastern slopes, and the western foot-hills, as well as those of the dry country in the south. He spared no one; everyone was put to death. This was what

the LORD God of Israel had commanded. . . . Joshua conquered all these kings and their territory in one campaign because the LORD, Israel's God, was fighting for Israel.

The stories of the conquest are not all the same. Some see only God winning victory. Then the armies of Israel just went in to mop up, after God had already confused the enemy and had won the battle. Other stories see the armies of Israel fighting more actively in battle.

Had Israel's beliefs changed? Did they no longer see God as their only warrior?

The oldest poem in Joshua and Judges is Judges 5, the Song of Deborah. This poem is among the oldest writings in the Bible. It was probably composed in the twelfth century B.C., and was in this form soon after the event it describes. In form, it is like many other victory songs of Egypt and Assyria. Unlike the Song of Moses, the Song of Deborah celebrates human action. The song praises the tribes that came to help Deborah and Barak. But the song is not like the victory songs of Egypt and Assyria, because it does not give credit for the victory to a king.

In the Song of Deborah, Yahweh is the leader of the battle. The song mentions Deborah more often than any other human leader, but her name appears only three times. Deborah also shares the glory with Barak, Jael, and the leaders of the various tribes that responded to the call to war.

The song does not mention any humans actually fighting in the battle. In Judges 5:20-21, stars fought against the kings of Canaan. A rainstorm flooded the Kishon Valley so that the chariots of the Canaanite army could not move through the water and mud. The song does not mention any Israelites fighting. In this song, the only person who killed another was Jael, who was not from Israel, but from the Kenite tribe. She killed Sisera, the leader of the Canaanite army, by hammering a tent peg through his head while he slept.

Scholars believe the prose version of the story (Joshua 4:4-22) was put together about two centuries later. It places more importance on fighting by the armies of Israel. But here, too, it was Jael who actually killed the enemy leader. It was God who threw into confusion the chariot soldiers of Sisera. Barak and his army merely chased and killed the already confused army of Sisera.

We can see that the people of Israel were fighting holy war in Canaan in a different way than in the Exodus. Now the armies of Israel were part of the fighting. But the story still points Israel away from depending on its own strength to win the battle, and instead depending on God to win for them.

CHAPTER 4

An Old-Fashioned Army

In many ways, war in early Israel was much like war in other parts of the Near East during the twelfth to tenth centuries B.C. The army of Israel had swords, shields, bows, and spears, like the armies of other nations of the time. But the army of Israel did not have horses and chariots, the up-to-date means of war that their neighbors used. The army of Israel was decidedly old-fashioned.

Israel did not use horses and chariots. This was not because they were too poor to have horses and chariots. Rather, they chose not to have them. After Joshua defeated Hazor and the other nations of the north, he cut the hamstrings of the horses and burned the chariots of his enemies. He did this because God told him to do it. (See Joshua 11:1-15.) Instead of trusting in modern weapons, Israel was to trust in God to win the battle.

Before the time of King Solomon, Israel had few chariots (1 Kings 9:19; 10:26). They were used only as private transportation for important people and in special ceremonies. In Israel, only Yahweh was to have chariots, and they were the clouds (Habbakuk 3:8; Psalm 68:17; Deuteronomy

32:13, literally, Yahweh "gives him the heights of the land to ride [on horse or chariot]").

At times, Israel even refused to use the weapons that they did have. Gideon and the army of Israel defeated the army of Midian with an unlikely combination of "weapons": trumpets and jars with a torch inside. Then while the army of Gideon was blowing their trumpets, Yahweh made the enemy troops attack each other with their swords. Only after the outcome of the battle was decided did Gideon and his men take their swords and chase the Midianites to capture their leaders. (See Judges 7.)

The crossing of the Jordan River (Joshua 3—4) was an act of war. Its story in the Bible uses war language and war images. The Ark of the Covenant led the way, just as it did in armed battle. The people were asked to make themselves clean, just as they would before battle. The people were dressed for battle (Joshua 4:12-13). Yet they used no weapons.

God got the credit for bringing them across the Jordan River on dry land, just as God had brought them out of Egypt through the Red Sea on dry land. God told the people of Israel who made a covenant with God at Shechem, "I gave you victory. . . . Your swords and bows had nothing to do with it" (Joshua 24:11-12).

Israel also refused to depend on large numbers of soldiers. When Gideon and his men prepared to fight the Midianites, God said to Gideon, "The men you have are too many for me to give them victory over the Midianites. They might think that they had won by themselves, and so give me no credit" (Judges 7:2). By sending home the twenty-two thousand who were afraid and the more than nine thousand who drank water on their knees, the army of

Gideon was reduced to only three hundred men. Yet God gave them victory over the Midianites, the Amalekites, and the desert tribesmen who "were spread out in the valley like a swarm of locusts, and they had as many camels as there are grains of sand on the seashore" (Judges 7:12).

Israel chose not to have a professional army—soldiers who were paid to fight. Instead, the army of early Israel was made up of volunteers. When a "judge" was called to go to war, he or she sent word to all the tribes to send volunteer soldiers to the battle. When the battle was over, the volunteers went home. The judge, or leader of the battle, also went home.

After the army of Gideon had defeated the Midianites, the Israelites tried to make Gideon and his son their rulers. Gideon answered, "I will not be your ruler, nor will my son. The LORD will be your ruler" (Judges 8:23). In order for God to be the ruler, human leadership was to last only a short time to meet the crisis.

Abimelech, the son of Gideon, did make himself king after the death of Gideon. But Judges 9 sees the death of Abimelech three years later as the result of God paying him back for his crimes. Early Israel did not have the kind of central organization that would give a human being credit for winning a war.

Israel practiced an old custom in the Near East called the "ban." This meant killing all the soldiers in a defeated enemy army plus the women and children—everyone—even the animals. It also meant burning all the possessions of the enemy that could be burned. Precious metals were usually saved. All these things were then "devoted" to the god of the winning side. The enemies and all their possessions became an offering to God. The practice seems cruel to us, but it was a way of making sure that soldiers on the winning side did not become rich by taking the possessions of the enemy, or by taking the enemy as slaves. So God was able to use for some good even one of the bloodiest practices of warfare in the ancient Near East.

Many of the customs of warfare in early Israel were more like those of cultures of the eighteenth century B.C. than like those of other twelfth- or eleventh-century cultures around Israel. They used old-fashioned means of warfare. It appears that Israel felt God did not want them to use modern weapons or modern ways of waging war. God was directing them toward depending on God rather than depending on weapons or large, paid armies or human rulers.

After entering Canaan, Israel no longer depended on God alone as completely as they had in the Exodus. They used weapons. They killed people. But they had faith not to make their army modern and to depend on God to save them in spite of their small numbers and old-fashioned weapons. They had faith not to have a human king and to let God be their ruler and commander-in-chief.

CHAPTER 5

God as Ruler

To have God as the only important warrior also meant to have God as ruler. In the ancient Near East, the king was not only the leader in war. He was also the political leader, the judge, the religious leader, and the owner of all or most of the land. Therefore, how a nation waged war was connected to how a nation acted in politics, religion, and economics. To say no to modern warfare was to say no to the kind of society that supported modern warfare.

Israel moved into a land of many small Canaanite city-states. These city-states were feudal, that is, they were ruled by kings and nobles who kept the people they ruled in forced labor. As these city-states developed in the sixteenth to thirteenth centuries B.C., war changed too.

To build and keep a chariot army meant that people needed to live closer together in cities with walls around them. Rulers were given more power. Warriors became a special class of people who oppressed a lower class. More taxes were taken from the people. For many farmers, higher taxes meant more debt. They were forced to sell their land to warriors of the upper class. Then they had to work as serfs for the upper class.

Into this setting came the people of Israel, who said, "God is our only ruler." Instead of having a central human ruler, Israel had temporary leaders, pressed into service for special purposes. All the tribes helped each other in time of battle. They also came together regularly for religious celebrations.

Before the time of Saul, there were no permanent leaders of Israel as a whole. Political power was scattered among the tribes. Each village had a council of elders who met at the city gate to make decisions, settle disputes, and witness contracts. Before the time of the kings, there was no upper class of chiefs.

Early Israel had no upper class and lower class. Most Israelites had about the same amount of resources. Modern excavations at the site of the ancient Israelite village of Tirzah show that houses of the tenth century B.C. are all of the same size and arrangement. Digging at a level of two centuries later, however, shows differences between the houses of the wealthy and the poor.

Each family in Israel was given land, which was to remain in the family. If poverty forced the family to sell the land, it was supposed to be redeemed (bought back) by a relative for the family. In the Jubilee Year (every forty-ninth or fiftieth year) all land went back to the families of the original owners at no cost. (See Leviticus 25.) As long as the Jubilee was practiced, it kept Israel from wide differences between rich and poor. Just as political power was spread out among the people, so was economic power.

This system of distributing land was connected to God as ruler. In theory, the ancient Near Eastern king was the owner of a large part of the land. He could give the land as he chose to his soldiers who had shown themselves to be loyal to him and had answered the call to war.

In Israel, however, God was the owner of all land (Leviticus 25:23). In Psalm 24, God's ownership of the whole world is connected with the idea of God as king and victorious warrior. Each Israelite family received its share of land from God. Their keeping the land was dependent on their staying loyal to God.

The major differences between Israel and Canaan were these: In Israel, all families received land, not just the upper class, as in Canaan. And Israel believed the real owner of the land was God, not a human king, as in Canaan.

Being part of early Israel was a matter of choice. Sometimes it appears that the armies of Israel came into Canaan, killed all the people who had been living there, and set up a new nation on their land. However, the biblical writers show that various other nations kept on living around the tribes of Israel for many years after Israel first crossed the Jordan River into Canaan. (See Judges 1:27-36.) Jerusalem was not taken by Israel until the time of King David.

At first, the nation of Israel did not have fixed boundaries that would have made everyone born and living within this area a part of Israel. The Jebusites, Perrizites, and Girgashites all lived in the same general area with the Israelites. Only under David and Solomon were all these peoples conquered and forced into the nation of Israel.

People from some other nations in the area could choose to become part of Israel. When the group of tribes from Egypt came into Canaan, they attracted a number of Canaanite people—such as Rahab and her family (Joshua 6:25) and the man from Bethel-Luz (Judges 1:22-26). Early

Israel was probably a mixture of people. Some came from Egypt (Exodus 12:38). Others were already in the area and liked the form of society in Israel and Israel's religion better than that of the Canaanite city-states.

So Israel's refusal to use "modern" warfare was part of a total way of living under God (Yahweh) as king. The Song of Moses ends, "You, LORD [Yahweh], will be king forever and ever" (Exodus 15:18). Gideon rejects being made king because "the LORD [Yahweh] will be your ruler" (Judges 8:23). In many of the Psalms, God is not only victorious warrior, but is giver of the land and is king. Psalm 47:2-4 says,

> The LORD, the Most High, is to be feared;
> he is a great king, ruling over all the world.
> He gave us victory over the peoples;
> he made us rule over the nations.
> He chose for us the land where we live,
> the proud possession of his people, whom he loves.

Like the ideal king of the Near East, Yahweh saves the people from their enemies. He rewards those who are loyal. He judges in favor of the oppressed, and gives food to the hungry. Like a good king,

> The LORD sets prisoners free
>   and gives sight to the blind.
> He lifts those who have fallen;
>   he loves his righteous people.
> He protects the strangers who live in our land;
>   He helps widows and orphans,
>   but ruins the plans of the wicked.

The LORD is king forever.
>Your God, Oh Zion, will reign for all time.
Praise the LORD. (Psalm 146:7d-10)

Elsewhere in the ancient Near East, the gods were seen as supporting the human king. The people all knew their place in society and stayed there. The gods saw to it. War in these societies was different. According to these societies, "God is on our side" meant "God will bless whatever the king is able to do for our nation."

The God of Israel, on the other hand, supported a society in which land and political power were shared among the people. The God of Israel did not affirm the power ambitions of a few. Instead, Yahweh asked Israel to give the central power to Yahweh alone. Israel was not to build up a powerful standing army. Israel was to depend on Yahweh for victory in war, and for keeping them in the land which had been promised to them.

CHAPTER 6

Give Us a King Like the Other Nations

By the eleventh century B.C., the nations around Israel were gaining strength in war. Israel felt especially pressed by the Philistines, a coastal people who were moving in from the west. Because the judge Samuel was growing old, the leaders of Israel went to him with a request. They said, "We want a king, so that we will be like other nations, with our own king to rule us and to lead us out to war and to fight our battles" (1 Samuel 8:19-20).

First Samuel 8—12 depicts God as letting Israel have a king only with great reluctance. To ask for a human king was to reject Yahweh as king. First Samuel 12:17 says that this asking for a king was a great sin against God. Samuel warned the people that they would be sorry later that they had asked for a king.

Samuel told them all the things that Near Eastern kings did to the people they ruled. The king would draft soldiers for a chariot army. He would make their sons and daughters work for him. He would tax their income to support his court officers. He would make them slaves (1 Samuel 8:10-18). But the people insisted on having a king. So Samuel poured oil on the head of Saul. That was the symbol that Saul had been chosen to be the king.

In 1 Samuel it is as if God was willing to work with the people of Israel even if they chose a king as their leader in government and in war. God allowed a situation that was not ideal. There was, at the same time, both a sense that to choose a king was to reject God, and that God had given them the king. Samuel told the people,

> Now here is the king you chose; you asked for him, and now the LORD has given him to you. All will go well with you if you honor the LORD your God, serve him, listen to him, and obey his commands, and if you and your king follow him. But if you do not listen to the LORD but disobey his commands, he will be against you and your king.... Even though you have done such an evil thing [to ask for a king], do not turn away from the LORD, but serve him with all your heart. Don't go after false gods; they cannot help you or save you, for they are not real. The LORD has made a solemn promise, and he will not abandon you, for he has decided to make you his own people. (1 Samuel 12:13-15, 20b-22)

Israel now had a king. But that king was not to be like the kings of the other nations. The Law of Kingship (Deuteronomy 17:14-20) commanded that the king not build up a large army with horses. The king was not to have many wives. That is, he was not to make treaties with other nations by marriage. This would mean that the foreign wives would bring with them the worship of other gods. He was not to make himself rich. Most important, he was to have a copy of the book of the laws of God and obey them faithfully. This would keep him from thinking that he was better than his fellow Israelites.

Also in the book of Deuteronomy (which was likely compiled during the time of the kings) are laws about war. These do not mention the king, but reflect the kind of holy war that Israel had before the time of the kings. It was still not important for the army of Israel to be large or to use modern ways of fighting. "When you go out to fight against your enemies and you see chariots and horses and an army that outnumbers yours, do not be afraid of them. The LORD your God, who rescued you from Egypt, will be with you" (Deuteronomy 20:1).

According to these laws about war, no one was forced to fight in battle. Anyone could go home who had just built a house, had just planted a vineyard, was engaged to be married, or was afraid. This meant that the army of Israel still had to depend on God to win for them (see Deuteronomy 20:1-20).

Most of the kings of Israel and of Judah did not follow these laws about kingship and war. But there are a few exceptions. The early stories of Saul and David show that the people relied more on God for victory. Jonathan won the battle at Michmash Pass in spite of the fact that only he and one other Israelite were fighting against the whole Philistine army (1 Samuel 14:1-15). David defeated the giant Goliath and the rest of the Philistines with only a slingshot. David told Goliath,

> You are coming against me with sword, spear, and javelin, but I come against you in the name of the LORD Almighty, the God of the Israelite armies, which you have defied. . . .

And everyone here will see that the LORD does not need swords or spears to save his people. He is victorious in battle, and he will put all of you in our power. (1 Samuel 17:45, 47)

But more and more, the king or the human warrior was given the credit for winning battles, not God. The women sang a victory song for David, not for God (1 Samuel 18:7). Instead of depending on a volunteer army, David had his own paid army. It fought separately from "all Israel," the volunteers. In most of the war stories, David is the main character.

Solomon made treaties with many other nations and, as a result, brought to Jerusalem many foreign wives. (Marriages between two royal families were a way of agreeing to keep international treaties.) These wives then had altars to their gods built in Jerusalem. Solomon built up a huge chariot army. The time of the kings was the most warlike period in Israel's history.

Under David and Solomon, Israel conquered large sections of land belonging to other nations and brought it under the control of Israel. Many people who worshiped other gods were considered to be part of Israel. Instead of one class of people, there were now rich and poor. The poor were not always treated kindly. The kings fought wars to defend themselves or to add more land to their kingdom. They were not as concerned about whether God would save them. They depended on their armies to save them.

After Solomon's death, Israel was divided into two kingdoms: Israel in the north and Judah in the south. They even fought each other. Later, both Israel and Judah fought against the superpowers of the Near East—Assyria and Babylon. The writer of 1 and 2 Kings thought that most of the kings had "sinned against the LORD." Only a few were considered good kings who obeyed God.

CHAPTER 7

The Prophets

The people who kept reminding Israel about God's law and God's kind of war were the prophets. As kings arose, so did prophets. Prophets were responsible for reminding the people and the king of their covenant with God. That responsibility included how to carry on war—and whether to go to war. The prophet not only gave the king advice when asked, but confronted the king when the king sinned.

Prophets could bring a word of warning to their own kings. Jehu told King Baasha of Israel that his whole family would die because he had sinned against God (1 Kings 16:1-4). Elijah told King Ahab that he had done wrong when he took over the vineyard of Naboth. He had violated the law which kept land in the same family from generation to generation (1 Kings 21).

A prophet could bring good news, too. The prophet Ahijah told Jeroboam that he would become king of the ten northern tribes when King Solomon died. He also said that a son of Solomon, Rehoboam, would rule over only one tribe. Thus, the word of the prophet gave permission for Jeroboam to rebel against the royal family (1 Kings 11:29-39).

On the other side of the conflict, the prophet Shemaiah told the word of God to Rehoboam and to the tribes of Judah and Benjamin. "Do not attack your own brothers, the people of Israel. Go home, all of you. What has happened is my will" (1 Kings 12:21-24).

The prophet Micaiah told King Ahab of Israel that he and King Jehoshaphat of Judah should not attack Syria, or Ahab would not come back alive (1 Kings 22). In 1 Kings 20, a prophet whose name we do not know told Ahab to attack the army of Syria. Prophets like Elisha evidently went along to war with the army so that, in times of decision, the kings could consult them. (See 2 Kings 3.)

Some prophets were employed by the king, and felt pressure to tell the king whatever he wanted to hear. But sometimes the prophets brought messages from God that were not favorable to the king. (See 1 Kings 22.)

Kingship in Israel and Judah did not mean that kings could do whatever they pleased. The law of God was above the king. The king was to have a copy of God's laws and teaching, to read from it all his life, and to obey faithfully everything that was commanded in it. (See Deuteronomy 17:18-19.) One of the things a prophet was to do was to keep constantly urging the king and the people back to obeying God's law.

In Jeremiah 1:9-10, the prophet was placed in authority over the nations instead of the warrior-king, as was the case in the ancient Near East. The prophet was Yahweh's chief political officer. His only basis of power was the word of God. For Jeremiah, law enforcement was not by violence, but by the law "written on the heart" (Jeremiah 31:33).

The prophet, not the king, was one who stood in the council of Yahweh. His task was to tell people the will and message of Yahweh as he had heard it in the heavenly assembly. (See Isaiah 6; 1 Kings 22; Jeremiah 23:18, 22.)

In many of these stories of kings and prophets, we do not see clearly the tradition of holy war that we found in the earlier stories. But in other stories, the prophet was clearly saying that God's people did not need to be afraid of the enemy; God would fight for them. The prophet kept calling people back to the ideal of holy war.

In holy war, the people and their leaders were to rely on God alone for the victory. They did not need large armies. They did not need modern weapons. God would work through their faith, not their military power. Isaiah said, "If your faith is not enduring, you will not endure" (Isaiah 7:9). He gave the king the word of God, "Come back and quietly trust in me. Then you will be strong and secure" (Isaiah 30:15). Then God would bring victory.

Sometimes this happened by miracles. When the king of Syria sent his army to capture Elisha, Elisha was saved by God's army of horses and chariots of fire. These were visible to the servant of Elisha only after Elisha prayed that he might see them (see 2 Kings 6:8-23). God saved the starving city of Samaria from the Syrian army by miracle rather than by military action. Second Kings 7:6-7 says,

> The Lord had made the Syrians hear what sounded like the advance of a large army with horses and chariots, and the Syrians thought that the king of Israel had hired Hittite and Egyptian kings and their armies to attack them. So that evening, the Syrians had fled for their lives, abandoning their tents, horses, and donkeys, and leaving the camp just as it was.

At other times, the message of the prophet was not to use modern weapons or to become an ally of nations with more modern military equipment. While two foreign armies attacked the city of Jerusalem, the prophet Isaiah advised King Hezekiah not to depend on the help of Egypt with its large numbers of horses, chariots, and soldiers. "Those who go to Egypt for help are doomed. . . . They do not rely on the LORD, the holy God of Israel, or ask him for help" (Isaiah 31:1).

During this period, it was usually assumed that war was a necessary part of being a nation. But some of the prophets also had a vision for a future day when all the world would be at peace. Isaiah spoke of days to come when many nations would come to the temple of the God of Israel to learn to walk in God's ways. Then God would settle disputes among nations. What the nations would do in the future, Judah was to do now. Isaiah said to them, "They will hammer their swords into plows and their spears into pruning knives. Nations will never again go to war, never prepare for battle again" (Isaiah 2:4).

People in Old Testament times also thought having a king was necessary for leading a nation in battle. As a whole, the prophets were not against kingship. They saw that God could use a king for God's own purposes. But the people who edited the books of Deuteronomy through 2 Kings saw that all but a few of the kings had not obeyed God. Again and again, the Scripture says about a king, "He, like his predecessors, sinned against the LORD. He followed the wicked example of King Jeroboam, son of Nebat, who led Israel into sin" (2 Kings 15:9 and elsewhere).

In theory, it was possible for God to use kingship for

good. But it usually did not happen that way. Kings usually did not follow the advice of the true prophets. They often allowed the worship of other gods besides the true God. They often did not trust the true God to save them from their enemies, but trusted instead in the superpowers of the day, Egypt or Assyria or Babylon. The prophets began telling kings and people: God will punish you for your sins. God will bring your defeat as a nation.

Thus, for about four hundred and fifty years, the people of Israel and Judah lived under kings. Afterward, they had to learn again how to be a nation without a human king. They learned that lesson through military defeat.

CHAPTER 8

The Other Side of Holy War

In 722 B.C., Samaria, the capital of the northern kingdom of Israel, fell to the armies of Assyria. The people were taken away to other Assyrian provinces. People of other defeated nations were brought in to populate the area where Israel had been. That was the end of kings in Israel.

In the southern kingdom of Judah, the capital city Jerusalem did not fall to Assyria immediately. Instead, Judah became a colony of Assyria and had to pay heavy taxes to Assyria. The kingdom of Judah lasted for another one hundred and fifty years before falling to the armies of Babylon in 587-586 B.C. However, only the leaders and the upper class of Judah were taken away to Babylon. Many of the common people were allowed to stay, but they had to live under a governor chosen by Babylon.

The prophets saw these defeats as punishment of Israel and Judah for being unfaithful to God. These defeats were really God fighting *against* God's people. Holy war was not an easy slogan, "God is on our side." Holy war was really God's war. If God's people did not obey the Law, God could and would fight against them.

In one sense, the people of Israel had always known that they needed to follow the way of God in order for God to keep fighting for them. They needed to obey the law of God in order to keep the land that God had given them.

Even while the people of Israel were wandering in the wilderness between Egypt and Canaan, Moses told them that, whenever they disobeyed God, Yahweh would not be with them. In Numbers 14:42-43, Moses told the armies of Israel:

> Don't go. The LORD is not with you, and your enemies will defeat you. When you face the Amalekites and the Canaanites, you will die in battle; the LORD will not be with you, because you have refused to follow him.

In Deuteronomy 28, the giving of the Law is completed. After this is a list of blessings and curses. The blessings were for when the people obeyed God and kept God's commandments. The curses were disasters that would fall on the people if they rejected God and the Law. (See also Leviticus 26:14-26.)

Even the presence of the Ark of the Covenant was not enough to prevent defeat if the people of Israel sinned. In 1 Samuel 4, the armies of Israel suffered defeat even after they brought the Ark of the Covenant into battle, because the sons of Eli had spoken evil against God.

Again, before the defeat of Judah and Israel, the prophets warned the people that they were sinning against God. Their sins, said the prophets, would bring punishment.

The prophets saw that the people were not obeying

God's covenant with them. The prophets were quite specific about the sins which the people were committing. Isaiah gave God's word to the people:

> You are doomed! You make unjust laws that oppress my people. That is how you keep the poor from having their rights and from getting justice. That is how you take the property that belongs to widows and orphans. What will you do when God punishes you? (Isaiah 10:1-3a)

You will be sent away to another country, said Isaiah, and only a few of you will ever come back.

Hosea said,

> There is no faithfulness or love in the land, and the people do not acknowledge me as God. They make promises and break them; they lie, murder, steal, and commit adultery. Crimes increase, and there is one murder after another. (Hosea 4:1-3)

Not only had the people been treating each other badly, they had been going to war in the wrong way: "Because you trusted in your chariots and in the large number of your soldiers, war will come to your people, and all your fortresses will be destroyed" (Hosea 10:13b-14a).

But most of all, according to Hosea, the people had forgotten the one true God:

> The LORD says, I am the LORD your God, who led you out of Egypt. You have no God but me. I alone am your savior. I took care of you in a dry, desert land. But when you entered the good land, you became full and satisfied, and then you grew proud and forgot me. So I will attack you like a lion. (Hosea 13:4-7)

The prophet Jeremiah told Judah that God would divorce them just as God had Israel, a figure of speech referring to Israel's defeat by Assyria (Jeremiah 3). The sin of Judah was worshiping gods that could do nothing for them, instead of the true God. "You refused to obey me and worship me. On every high hill and under every green tree you worshiped fertility gods," God told the people through Jeremiah (Jer. 2:20).

Micah warned the people who were building Jerusalem on murder and injustice.

> The city's rulers govern for bribes, the priests interpret the Law for pay, the prophets give their revelations for money—and they all claim that the LORD is with them. "No harm will come to us," they say. "The LORD is with us." (Micah 3:11)

But simply saying "Yahweh is with us," was no protection for those who had broken the law of God.

When people try to worship without doing justice, God will not listen, says Isaiah 1.

> Wash yourselves clean. Stop all this evil that I see you doing. Yes, stop doing evil and learn to do right. See that justice is done—help those who are oppressed, give orphans their rights, and defend widows.... If you will only obey me, you will eat the good things the land produces. But if you defy me, you are doomed to die. I, the LORD, have spoken. (Isaiah 1:16-17, 19-20)

The penalty for the people's turning away from God was defeat and destruction at the hands of the armies of Assyria and Babylon.

CHAPTER 9

God Chose
Other Armies

So, who were the soldiers of God now, since God was no longer with Israel and Judah? According to the prophet Isaiah, God chose foreign armies to correct wayward Israel and Judah:

> The LORD has called out his proud and confident soldiers to fight a holy war and punish those he is angry with. Listen to the noise on the mountains—the sound of a great crowd of people, the sound of nations and kingdoms gathering. The LORD of Armies is preparing his troops for battle. They are coming from far-off countries at the ends of the earth. In his anger the LORD is coming to devastate the whole country (Isaiah 13:3-5).

In this case, God used the army of Assyria to bring about God's purpose for Judah.

The army of Assyria was certainly not godly. In fact, Assyria had one of the most brutal armies in the ancient Near East. The Assyrians had quite a reputation for being violent even when it was not necessary. When the

Assyrians defeated a country, they took the population away and scattered them among many other nations which they had defeated. Then they brought people from those other nations to settle the territory.

The Assyrians not only killed people they would not have had to kill; they also destroyed any chance of the people becoming a nation again. That is what happened to the northern kingdom of Israel.

We cannot say that God liked the way Assyria behaved. There is nothing in the Bible that points to the king of Assyria worshiping Yahweh, the God of the Israelites. In fact, in the same chapter in which God calls Assyria "the rod of my anger" with which God will attack Judah, God also foretells judgment: "When I finish what I am doing on Mount Zion and in Jerusalem, I will punish the emperor of Assyria for all his boasting and all his pride" (Isaiah 10:12).

Certainly, God did not approve of the way Assyria acted. Yet, in spite of their cruelty, God used their army to defeat Israel and Judah for their good. The emperor of Assyria probably did not know that God would use him for good. But God could use even the Assyrian defeat of the people of Israel to lead them back to worshiping Yahweh only.

The prophet Isaiah saw that God dealt this way, not only with Judah, but with all nations. God would punish the emperor of Assyria for his boasting that "I have done it all myself" (Isaiah 10:13ff.). In chapters 13—25, Isaiah gave God's message that Babylon, Assyria, Moab, Syria, Philistia, Sudan, Egypt, Arabia, and Phoenicia would all be punished for their sins. No nation would escape. God would hold them all accountable for what they did.

Ezekiel prophesied against not only Judah, but the nations around it (see chapters 25—32). Ezekiel heard God saying to the king of Tyre, "Because you think you are as wise as a god, I will bring ruthless enemies to attack you" (Ezekiel 28:6-7).

So Israel and Judah learned a lesson through national defeat. They learned that they could not expect that God would always be on their side in war just because God had made a covenant with them. If the people of God broke their side of the covenant, they would lose the blessings of the covenant. If they no longer acted as though God were their ruler, then God would no longer treat them as loyal subjects.

The same applied to other nations, too. Any people who did not trust in God would find that God the Warrior sometimes fought against them.

CHAPTER 10

The Mercy of God

But the story does not end there. God wanted to do more than just punish nations that had sinned. God wanted the people to stop doing wrong and turn again to God as their ruler. God wanted a new relationship with the people.

Isaiah said that the punishment for sin was like a fire that a silversmith might use to purify precious metal. Then Israel or Judah would be free from impurities (sins) and could come under the covenant of God again. (See Isaiah 1:24-27.)

God wanted people to change and begin doing good again. Jeremiah was distressed at the sin he saw among the people and at the disaster he saw coming to them. He did not want that disaster to occur. So he told the people worshiping in the temple in Jerusalem that God was saying: "Change the way you are living and stop doing the things you are doing. Be fair in your treatment of each other. Stop taking advantage of aliens, orphans, and widows. Stop killing innocent people in this land. Stop worshiping other gods, for that will destroy you. *If you change,* I will let you go on living here in the land which I

gave to your ancestors as a permanent possession"
(Jeremiah 7:5-7, italics mine).

Hosea 1—3 gives a vivid picture of how God punishes
Israel, but also wants Israel to come back to God. In these
chapters, God is compared to a husband whose wife, Israel,
has been unfaithful, running with other lovers. Because she
has rejected her marriage relationship, the husband di-
vorces her. But at the same time, he goes out into the
wilderness to woo her back with words of love. He wants to
marry her again, if she will return. He loves her and is willing to make a new covenant of peace with her.

In Hosea 5:15, God says, "I will abandon my people
until they have suffered enough for their sins and come
looking for me. Perhaps in their suffering they will try to
find me."

Even though it looked as if God would destroy the
people of Israel by defeat in war, God really wanted the
people to come back into right relationship. God was really
the ruler over all. Just as God could use victory in war to
make Israel a nation, God could also use defeat in war as a
way to persuade the people to turn back to being subjects
of the one true God.

God wanted to save all nations. The warnings of punishment for other nations were not the end of the story for
them any more than for Israel.

After the prophet Isaiah spoke his words of warning and
disaster for all the rulers of the earth, he also spoke of a
time when all nations would recognize God as their ruler
on Mount Zion:

> Here on Mount Zion the LORD Almighty [commander of
> armies] will prepare a banquet for all the nations of the
> world—a banquet of the richest food and the finest wine.

Here he will suddenly remove the cloud of sorrow that has been hanging over all the nations. The Sovereign LORD will destroy death forever! He will wipe away the tears from everyone's eyes and take away the disgrace his people have suffered throughout the world. The LORD himself has spoken. When it happens, everyone will say, "He is our God! We have put our trust in him, and he has rescued us. He is the LORD! We have put our trust in him, and now we are happy and joyful because he has saved us." (Isaiah 25:6-9)

The God who uses war to save the people of God, and war to bring disaster, is also the same God who loves people and wants them to return to a rightful relationship. God wants a new covenant with people who will trust in God alone to save them from their enemies.

CHAPTER 11

Hope for God's Victory

The people of Judah were in exile in faraway Babylon. They had no human Jewish king. They had no army. How could God still be the ruler over all nations, and the powerful warrior when the people of God were being persecuted and killed? How could they sing God's songs, the songs of Zion, in a foreign land? Could they worship a God who had not saved them from their enemies? Were they supposed to rise in hopeless revolution against the government that was oppressing them?

During almost all of the period from the fall of Jerusalem in 587 B.C. through New Testament times, the Jewish people lived under foreign rule. Even after Cyrus, the emperor of Persia, defeated Babylon and allowed some of the Jews to go back to Jerusalem in 538 B.C., the people of Judah were not an independent nation. They still lived under Persian rule. Later, they lived under Greek rule, beginning in 333 B.C. After 63 B.C., the Romans occupied Palestine. Only from 166 to 63 B.C. was there an independent Jewish state, established after the revolt led by Judas Maccabeus.

God had brought them out of Egypt. God had created a nation from a group of slaves. God had brought them through the wilderness to the promised land. They no longer had their own land—or at least, little control over it. How could the Jews continue to be a people?

The Jewish people developed a twofold response to living under foreign rule. Their first response was nonviolent resistance. They were not to go to war against their oppressors. They would live under a foreign government peacefully, insofar as possible. But they would refuse to do anything that would mean worshiping a god other than Yahweh. The second side of the Jewish response was to have faith that someday—soon or in the distant future—God would come to save the people of God. They did not have to depend on their being strong in war; God would free them from their oppressors.

Daniel 1—6 shows the first response most clearly. The book of Daniel was written during a time of persecution, possibly during the time when the Greeks ruled Palestine. The book of Daniel intends to give the people of God the courage to endure persecution and to trust in God, just as Daniel and his friends did.

This first part of the book tells of a group of young Jews in exile who had taken seriously the advice of Jeremiah to work for the good *(shalom)* of the city of Babylon (Jeremiah 29:7). At least four of them had agreed to work in the government of Babylon. They were serving in the court of King Nebuchadnezzar.

Even though they were serving a foreign king, they did not obey his laws which were in conflict with the laws of God. Daniel and his friends refused to eat food that was ritually unclean according to Jewish law (Daniel 1). His

friends refused to bow down and worship the gold statue
the king had built. As a result, the king threw them into a
blazing furnace. But an angel (a messenger of God) was
with them in the flames, and they came out of the fire
unharmed. Even the king recognized that God had been at
work here. He said:

> Praise the God of Shadrach, Meshach, and Abednego! He
> sent his angel and rescued these men who serve and trust
> him. They disobeyed my orders and risked their lives rather
> than bow down and worship any god except their own. . . .
> There is no other god who can rescue like this. (Daniel 3:28-
> 29)

Daniel prayed to his God three times a day, even though
it violated the law of King Darius. The king had Daniel
thrown into a pit of lions, but God sent an angel to shut the
mouths of the lions. "So they pulled him [Daniel] up and
saw that he had not been hurt at all, for he trusted God"
(Daniel 6:23). This trust in God to save them helped unite
the Jews in spite of persecution.

When a minority group within a society is oppressed, it
must resist the majority culture to survive as a people. Yet
the minority group does not have to say no to everything in
the majority culture. Daniel and his friends could be
government workers in Babylon. But they had to sometimes say no to keep their separate Jewish identity.

Worshiping other gods, for example, seems to have been
a large issue. But they also said no to things which may
seem to us to be a small point, such as the food laws. They
carefully chose when to say no (without violence). That
was enough to help them remain a separate people

worshiping their own God. They did not start a revolution, but the Jews (at least, some of them) resisted being drawn into the Babylonian mainstream. They simply remained a minority group within Babylonian society. God would still be their king, even though they were living in Babylon.

The second part of the Jewish response was to wait for God to save them. Even while they were in Babylon, they kept alive the hope that God the Warrior would win out over the enemies. The Jews had the hope that God would destroy their oppressors and bring God's own people back to Palestine. The book of Zechariah speaks of God the Warrior fighting to allow the exiles to return to Jerusalem:

> So the LORD Almighty [Yahweh, commander of armies] sent me with this message for the nations that had plundered his people: "The LORD himself will fight against you, and you will be plundered by the people who were once your servants." (Zechariah 2:8-9)

The prophets used the language of holy war when they spoke about God bringing back the Jewish nation. But they used this language in a way more like Moses in the Exodus than like King David. In the Exodus from Egypt, the people of God did not have to use weapons. They could just march across the Red Sea and let God fight for them. So now, the prophets of an oppressed people talked again about God fighting for them. The war was Yahweh's. Yahweh had all the weapons. Like the Israelite slaves escaping from Egypt, the Jews had only to be calm and to wait for the salvation of God.

The book of Habbakuk describes the coming of God like a warrior, riding on the clouds. "The storm cloud was your chariot, as you brought victory to your people" (Habbakuk 3:8b). God, the victorious warrior, would again be king. "The Sovereign LORD is coming to rule with power, bringing with him the people he has rescued. He will take care of his flock like a shepherd" [a Near-Eastern term for the king] (Isaiah 40:10-11a).

The war cry of Yahweh ("Do not be afraid. I am with you") resounds from the prophets of this period. Isaiah says:

> Do not be afraid—I am with you! I am your God—let nothing terrify you! I will make you strong and help you; I will protect you and save you. Those who are angry with you will know the shame of defeat. Those who fight against you will die and will disappear from the earth. I am the LORD your God; I strengthen you and tell you, "Do not be afraid; I will help you." (Isaiah 41:10-13)

The prophet cried to God, reminding God of how God saved the people of Israel in the past, in creation, in the Exodus:

> Wake up, LORD, and help us! Use your power to save us: use it as you did in ancient times. It was you that cut the sea monster Rahab to pieces. It was you also who dried up the sea and made a path through the water, so that those you were saving could cross. (Isaiah 51:9-10)

Daniel 7 affirms that someday the "one who has been living forever" will win out over evil governments. The people of God, who were now oppressed, would also be winners. "Then the one who had been living forever came and pronounced judgment in favor of the people of the

Supreme God. The time had arrived for God's people to receive royal power" (Daniel 7:22). The people of God would then have a new king, a "son of man." He would be given "authority, honor and royal power, so that the people of all nations, races, and languages would serve him. His authority would last forever, and his kingdom would never end" (Daniel 7:14).

The prophets looked forward to the "Day of the Lord," or the "Day of Yahweh," the phrase used to describe holy war. This was the time when God the Warrior would come to save those who were faithful to God, and to punish those who had disobeyed God. The prophet Joel saw the disaster of locusts coming upon the fields as a sign that the Day of Yahweh was coming soon. "The LORD thunders commands to his army. The troops that obey him are many and mighty. How terrible is the day of the LORD! Who will survive it?" (Joel 2:11).

But the Day of Yahweh was not only a day of disaster, when the people who were not on the side of Yahweh would get the punishment they deserved. It was also a day of mercy. Yahweh wanted people to repent and return to worshiping the true God. God was kind and full of mercy. God was always ready to forgive and not punish, said Joel.

God was the redeemer, the next-of-kin, who would pay the price to rescue his relatives, the people of Israel, from slavery.

Toward the end of the book of Isaiah, we find a picture of the Servant of Yahweh who will save the people in a gentle way. In some passages, the Servant seems to be a single person. In other passages, the Servant seems to be the whole nation of Israel.

Alongside the image of God as a warrior, attacking the

enemy, is the image of the Servant of God who will bring justice to every nation. This will happen not through military means, but quietly, gently. He will not "break off a bent reed nor put out a flickering lamp" (Isaiah 42:3). His only sword is his word which he speaks (Isaiah 49:2).

The Servant will, in fact, suffer torture, insults, and death. By enduring suffering on behalf of others, the Servant will save them. Because the Servant fights not by destroying others, but by suffering on their behalf, God will "give him a portion with the great, and he shall divide the spoils with the strong" (Isaiah 53:12, NIV).

This is holy war language! The Servant has won. But what a way to win—gently enduring suffering!

CHAPTER 12

A Vision of Peace for All Nations

In this period of living under foreign government, the prophets received a vision: God really wanted peace for all nations. God was not only interested in saving the people of Israel. God wanted to save all people. God wanted all people to live in peace.

The prophets had said earlier that God would punish the foreign nations for their sins, just as God had punished Israel and Judah. During this time of oppression, the prophets were also saying that God wanted all people to repent of their sins, to worship God, and to live in peace.

After God as king won the victory, there would be no more war among the nations of the world. "Rejoice, Zion, your king is coming triumphant and victorious," said the prophet Zechariah. "I will remove the war chariots and horses. Your King will make peace among the nations" (Zechariah 9:9).

Isaiah also sees foreigners as well as the handicapped coming to the temple of God to offer sacrifices. "My temple will be called a house of prayer for the people of all nations" (Isaiah 56:7). This passage echoes the vision of

Isaiah 2: The nations would come streaming to the temple in Jerusalem, promising to do what Israel's God wanted them to do. They would let God "settle disputes among great nations. They will hammer their swords into plows and their spears into pruning knives. Nations will never again go to war, never prepare for battle again" (Isaiah 2:4). These prophets said that peace (*shalom*, which means "health, wholeness, and living in harmony with each other") was the real purpose which God had for humankind.

PART TWO

Holy War
in the New Testament

CHAPTER 13

Holy War Language in the New Testament

The language and theology of holy war continues into the New Testament. It often repeats the war cry, "Do not be afraid. I am with you."

Even the stories of the birth of Jesus include this war cry. When the angel appeared to Joseph, he said, "Do not be afraid to take Mary to be your wife" (Matthew 1:20-23). Then the Gospel writer quotes Isaiah about the son who is to be called *Immanuel*, "God-Is-With-Us." Angels repeated this war cry to Zechariah (Luke 1:13), to Mary (Luke 1:30), and to the shepherds (Luke 2:10).

The Gospels constantly use political language to talk about who Jesus was and what he was to do. They see Jesus as a king. They talk about the kingdom of God or the kingdom of heaven. Even the name *Jesus* (in its Hebrew form, *Joshua*) means "savior, deliverer, the leader of the liberation army."

Jesus showed people the saving power of God in two ways. The first way was through his miracles which showed

God's power over sickness, unclean spirits, sin, and death—all the evil forces and powers in the world that controlled people. The second way was through his teaching and his example of how to relate to human enemies.

The healings and other miracles in the Gospels are often called "signs" or "wonders" (see John 4:48). These are the words used in the story of the Exodus from Egypt to refer to the saving acts of God the Warrior (Deuteronomy 6:22 and elsewhere). By the "finger of God," Jesus drove out demons (Luke 11:20), just as, through Moses, the "finger of God" brought disaster on the Egyptians (Exodus 8:19) and gave the law on Mount Sinai (Exodus 31:18).

God did these miracles through Jesus in the same way that God, in ancient Israel, brought victory in war: through people's faith. In holy war, the armies of Israel were to trust in God, not in their weapons or their own skill. In the miracles, it was people's faith that saved them. In the story of the healing of the daughter of Jarius, Jesus gave the holy war cry to Jarius, "Don't be afraid; only believe [have faith], and she will be well" [literally, "be saved"] (Luke 8:50).

After Jesus had healed the blind Bartimaeus, Jesus told him, "Go, your faith has made you well" [has saved or liberated you] (Mark 10:52). In these miracles, the battle was against unclean spirits and the forces of sin and destruction.

People saw the miracles and made the connection between the battles of Jesus and the battles of ancient Israel. They saw the connection between military power and political power.

We can see this in John's report after Jesus had fed the five thousand:

> Seeing this miracle that Jesus had performed, the people there said, "Surely this is the Prophet who was to come into the world!" Jesus knew that they were about to come and seize him in order to make him king by force; so he went off again to the hills by himself. (John 6:14-15)

The crowds shouted their approval of Jesus as king, as he entered Jerusalem. The Gospel of John quotes Zechariah 9:9, a prophet of hope for the future rule of God: "Do not be afraid, city of Zion! Here comes your king, riding on a young donkey" (John 12:14-15).

Through Jesus, God was not only saving people from sin and unclean spirits, but from their human enemies as well. The Jewish people hoped not only for salvation from personal evil, but also from their Roman oppressors. Some of Jesus' disciples were Zealots, members of a Jewish political group that wanted to use force to drive the Romans out of Palestine.

The song of Mary celebrated the hope that God was saving her people from their enemies. "He has stretched out his mighty arm [see Exodus 6:6] and scattered the proud with all their plans. He has brought down mighty kings from their thrones and lifted up the lowly" (Luke 1:51-52).

Unlike the first Joshua, Jesus did not use human armies to help defeat the enemy. Jesus chose the best of the holy-war tradition: not the part in which the armies of Israel helped God win by fighting, but the part in which the people of Israel trusted God to do the fighting (Exodus 14:14; Isaiah 7:4; 30:15).

Jesus knew that there would be enemies and that the people who followed him would have to suffer or even be killed. But the power by which God would defeat the enemy was the power of love. The followers of Jesus did not have to be afraid of the enemy (Matthew 10:28), but could proclaim the gospel before rulers and kings (Mark 13:9-13).

When Jesus himself was arrested, he told Peter to put away the sword he had brought to defend Jesus (John 18:11). He told Pilate, the Roman governor, that in the kingdom of God, his followers did not fight (John 18:36). Jesus did his fighting like the Suffering Servant of Isaiah 53—gently, nonviolently, lovingly.

Jesus allowed himself to be killed rather than fight back with weapons, because he had faith that even his death would not keep God from winning the victory. This is what happened in the resurrection. The most important miracle was that God raised Jesus from the dead. This proved to the followers of Jesus that the Day of the Lord had come, and God was saving the people of God.

In his sermon on the Day of Pentecost, Peter quoted the passage from Joel and the signs and wonders that were to happen on the Day of the Lord. The Day of the Lord had come, Peter said. Now was the time for people to turn away from their sins and become part of the people of God. The raising of Jesus from the dead proved that God had won the battle over sin and death (Acts 2).

The rest of the New Testament also uses the language of holy war. In Acts, the apostle Paul had visions in which God told him not to be afraid to teach in Corinth, or to give his witness in Rome (Acts 18:9-11; 23:11). Ephesians 6:10-20 teaches us to put on the whole armor of God. "For we are not fighting against human beings, but against the wicked spiritual forces in the heavenly world; the rulers, authorities, and cosmic powers of this dark age." The only sword Christians are to have is the Word of God. The effect of putting on this armor is boldness in speaking about the gospel. First John 5:4 says, "Every child of God is able to defeat the world. And we win the victory over the world by means of our faith." Even in suffering, Christians were not to fear their oppressors nor to pay back evil with evil, but to honor Christ as Lord (1 Peter 3:9, 14-15).

Both the Gospels and Letters draw upon the vision of the prophets that someday there will be peace among people of all nations. Jesus healed Gentiles as well as Jews. The early church decided to include Gentiles—and slaves and women. Christ Jesus brought peace by breaking down the wall between Gentiles and Jews, and making them one people (Ephesians 2:13-15). The church was an example to the world of what peace was really like.

The language of holy war is especially common in the book of Revelation. Written during a time when the government was persecuting Christians, Revelation expresses hope in the future, final victory of God. The hero, Jesus, is seen as a gentle lamb whose sword is the sword of his mouth, his word (Revelation 2:16).

"Don't be afraid," says this Son of Man in Revelation 1:17-18. "I am the first and the last. I am the living one! I was dead, but now I am alive forever and ever. I have authority over death and the world of the dead." The Spirit says to the church in Smyrna,

> Don't be afraid of anything you are about to suffer. Listen! The Devil will put you to the test by having some of you thrown into prison, and your troubles will last ten days. Be faithful to me, even if it means death, and I will give you life as your prize of victory. (Revelation 2:10)

So, from Genesis to Revelation, the Bible draws on the theme of holy war. From the Exodus of the Hebrew slaves from Egypt, to the suffering of the church in the Roman world, the call to holy war is a call to trust in God. It is a call to trust in the power of God. It is a call to trust in the ways of God, not human ways.

CHAPTER 14

How God Used Holy War

In the history of Israel, we can see changes in the ways people thought they should deal with their enemies. In early times, war, and even practices like the ban, were accepted. In the exile, the message was to live with suffering but to say no nonviolently to the religion of Babylon. But no matter what the situation, God was able to use it to point toward better ways of dealing with enemies.

In the Old Testament, the people of Israel found themselves in a culture in which men had all the economic power. The Law of God did not tell people to remove themselves from their traditional culture. Instead, the Law used and transformed the culture to rise above male dominance and foster a special concern for the widow, the orphan, and the stranger. These were the people who had no adult Hebrew male to support them.

The people of Israel found themselves surrounded by nations with kings. God did not really want the people to have a human king. However, God was able to use kingship to develop a society in which the king was to be a student of the Law of God, just like everyone else. The king was to be a part of the community, not above it.

In the same way, the people of Israel found themselves in a culture in the ancient Near East that accepted holy war as the way to deal with national enemies. God did not ask people to come out of their culture. God did not tell the people of early Israel to stop going to war any more than God told them to stop speaking Hebrew. Instead, God defined holy war in such a way that the people of God were asked to trust God to do all the fighting.

The prophets kept asking people to depend on God alone. Through the prophets, God kept directing people to the real way that God acted: asking people to repent of their sins so God could show them love and mercy. The prophets kept reminding people of the real purpose of God: that all nations would come to know and worship God, become part of the people of God, and live together in peace.

Throughout the history of Israel, God took whatever evil practices God found and used them for good. God made people's sin into an opportunity for showing mercy and forgiveness. God used defeat by the brutal Assyrian army as a message to those who kept on sinning. God used warfare to lead people toward love and nonviolence. God was always able to take what was there, use it for good, and then ask people to move beyond it into God's better way of doing things.

CHAPTER 15

The Meaning of Holy War

What lessons for the present can we learn from this survey of holy war in the Bible? Here are some summary points to consider.

We can depend on God to save us from our enemies. Just as the Hebrew people escaping from Egypt had only to stand still and watch God fight for them, so we can trust God to fight enemies on our behalf. We, ourselves, do not need to fight. We do not need to make or buy bigger and better weapons to prepare to fight, or to threaten to fight. The power of God is great enough to win over all our enemies.

If we do not trust in God to save us from our enemies, we become idolaters. If we do not worship God as our only ruler, as the only one who can save us, then we turn something else into a god in the hope that it will save us. The kings of Israel trusted in their chariots and horses. We sometimes trust in modern weapons or military alliances with powerful countries to save us, rather than trust in God and God's ways of dealing with enemies.

How we relate to our enemies is a question of who we

think is really in control of the world. If we think that evil
forces and evil people are really in control, then we will try
to get rid of them if we think we are equally powerful. Or if
we think we are weak, we may be afraid of these evil
forces. The Old Testament tells us that we do not have to
have a strong army. Nor must we be afraid. God is already
on our side, fighting for us in God's own way. If God is
really our God, then we can trust God to liberate us from
the power of evil forces and evil people.

*We can trust in the power of God, not in human vio-
lence.* The other nations of the ancient Near East thought
that "God is on our side" meant that God would help them
fight with their own swords. They thought that God would
act through their fighting.

Holy war in Israel, however, teaches that God does not
work through our physical strength, but through our faith
in God. It is not important how many we are or how strong
we are, but how much we are able to trust in God and not
be afraid of the enemy. Even when Israel had armies, God
won the battle through the faith of the three hundred
soldiers of Gideon—not through their military strength.

In Isaiah 40—66, the prophet says that God will bring
victory through the Servant of God who suffers in faith,
rather than bringing suffering upon others. The Jews, suffering under foreign rule, had faith that God would do battle with both human and cosmic powers, and free them
someday. We can trust that, even if we die, God will overcome in the end, and we will see that God and the people
of God are the real winners. In the later parts of the Old
Testament, we see the beginnings of the idea that suffering
for the sake of God is the way to victory.

We can trust that someday God will bring a final victory

over all evil. The present suffering of the people of God is not the last word. Someday it will be clear to everyone that God is the real ruler of the world, with power over all other forces that claim to be in control. If we believe in the final victory of God over evil forces, then we should be willing to wait for it. We do not have to try to hurry up God's victory by causing suffering to our present enemies, or by killing them.

If we are confident that God will win in the end, then we can be calm now and wait for the salvation of God. No matter how bad things seem now, we know what will happen in the end. We do not have to use evil means to fight against evil forces. We can use the ways of God to deal with evil because we know the final outcome.

God as warrior is only one image of God in the Bible. The Old Testament uses many other word-pictures of God. God is also redeemer, our next-of-kin who buys us out of slavery. God is a loving husband who wants his unfaithful wife to return to faithfulness and marriage. God is a mother eagle who carefully teaches her young to fly. The Wisdom of God is a hostess inviting everyone to come to her banquet, even if they cannot pay. God is a father. God is fire. God is light. God is ruler. God is a shepherd. God is a potter. God is a rock of strength. The list goes on and on.

Some of these images are more important than others in the Old Testament. The image of God as warrior appears throughout the Bible. But no single image gives us the whole picture of what God is like and of God's way of peacemaking. If we have only one image of God, our picture is distorted. Then we are in danger of limiting God to the shape of our favorite image.

The commandment, "Do not make for yourselves

images" (Exodus 20:4), requires that we do not pick one image—warrior, potter, father, or golden calf—and call that God. We need many images by which to see God and, even then, we still can never understand the whole of God.

God wants all the people of the world to come to be part of the people of God. The vision of the prophets is for all nations to come streaming to Zion, the place of the worship of God. Then there will be peace. The people of God are not just those whose ancestors have known God, but all people who now know God, including the foreigner.

"People of God" does not follow the world's political boundaries. "People of God" includes men and women from around the world—everyone who worships the true God. The political loyalties of these people are to God and the people of God, not to the Nebuchadnezzars of the world claiming control. How can we fight against those who are also part of God's nation?

If we are part of the people of God, then we will share God's vision: A new community of people of every tribe and language beating their swords into plows and their spears into pruning knives. We can envision a community of God never preparing for war again, but using what were once the weapons of war to produce food for humankind.

God has a purpose for humankind. God wants all people to trust in God for their security. God wants all people to let God win the battle against evil for them—in God's way. God wants all people to live at peace in the community of God.

For Further Reading and Study

For Easier Reading:
Eller, Vernard. *War and Peace from Genesis to Revelation.* Scottdale, Pa., and Kitchener, Ont.: Herald Press, 1981. (Also published in 1973 as *King Jesus' Manual for Arms for the 'Armless.)*

For More Serious Study:
Craigie, Peter C. *The Problem of War in the Old Testament.* Grand Rapids, Mich.: Eerdmans, 1978.

Hanson, Paul D. *The Diversity of Scripture: A Theological Interpretation.* Philadelphia: Fortress Press, 1982. (This deals with the broader issues of biblical interpretation.)

Lind, Millard. *Yahweh Is a Warrior: The Theology of Warfare in Ancient Israel.* Scottdale, Pa., and Kitchener, Ont.: Herald Press, 1980.

Miller, Patrick D., Jr. *The Divine Warrior in Early Israel.* Cambridge, Mass.: Harvard University Press, 1973.

von Rad, Gerhard. *Der heilige Krieg im alten Israel.* Goettingen: Vandenhoeck & Ruprecht, 1952. (Soon to be translated into English.)

Yoder, John H. *The Politics of Jesus.* Grand Rapids, Mich.: Eerdmans, 1972. Especially Chapter 4.

The Author

Lois Barrett is mentor (teaching minister) for a cluster of house churches in Wichita, Kansas, known as Mennonite Church of the Servant. She also represents her congregation on Churches United for Peacemaking, a local organization of congregations working toward world peace.

Lois was born in Enid, Oklahoma, and raised in the home of a Christian Church (Disciples of Christ) minister. After completing high school in Sweetwater, Texas, she graduated from the University of Oklahoma in Norman. While at the University, she began to be involved in protests against the war in Vietnam. She went to Wichita in 1969 as a Mennonite Voluntary Service worker. It was there she became acquainted with Mennonites, and found a church that was clearly for peace in the world.

Since joining the Mennonite Church in 1971, Lois has been a member of a Christian intentional community (1971-78), has served as associate editor of *The Mennonite*, as news service director for the General Conference Mennonite Church (1971-77), and as editor of *The House Church* newsletter (1978-80; 83-85).

She has worked on peace issues through Churches United for Peacemaking (1983 to present), as a member-at-large of the Mennonite Central Committee U.S. Peace Section (1980-83), and as a member of the central planning committee of New Call to Peacemaking, a cooperative effort of historic peace churches in the United States (1977-80).

She currently serves on the executive council of the Institute of Mennonite Studies. She is the author of *The Vision and the Reality* (Faith and Life Press, 1983), *Building the House Church* (Herald Press, 1986), and numerous magazine articles.

In 1980-83, Lois completed her seminary education at Associated Mennonite Biblical Seminaries, Elkhart, Indiana. She returned to Wichita to minister with Mennonite Church of the Servant. She and her husband, Thomas Mierau, have three children, Barbara, Susanna, and John.

PEACE AND JUSTICE SERIES

Edited by Elizabeth Showalter and J. Allen Brubaker

This series sets forth briefly and simply some of the important emphases of the Bible on war and peace and how to deal with conflict and injustice. The authors write from within the Anabaptist tradition. This includes viewing the Scriptures as a whole as the believing community discerns God's word through the guidance of the Spirit.

Some of the titles reflect biblical, theological, or historical content; other titles in the series show how these principles and insights are practiced in daily life.

1. *The Way God Fights* by Lois Barrett.
2. *Early Christian Understandings of War* by John Driver.
3. *They Loved Their Enemies* by Marian Hostetler.

The books in this series are published in North America by:

Herald Press
616 Walnut Avenue
Scottdale, PA 15683
USA

Herald Press
117 King Street, West
Kitchener, ON N2G 4M5
CANADA

Overseas persons wanting copies for distribution or permission to translate may write to the Scottdale address listed above.